BE YOUR BEST SELF

LIFE SKILLS FOR UNSTOPPABLE KIDS

Button
BOOKS

**DANIELLE BROWN
AND NATHAN KAI**

CONTENTS

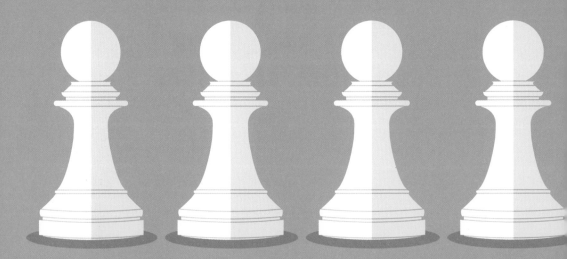

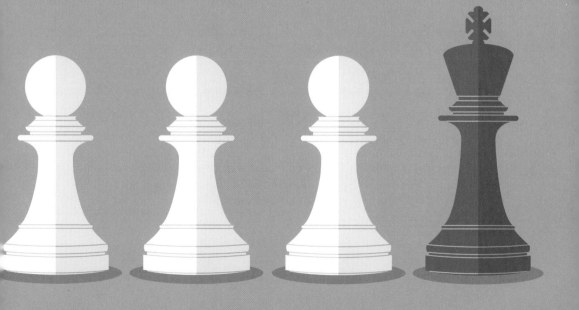

INTRODUCTION

We believe that every human being on this planet has the potential to achieve brilliant things. But how do you do it? How do you get from where you are right now to becoming the best possible version of yourself?

This is a question that Nathan asked himself a lot when he was seven years old.

Nathan's dream is to become a public speaker, travel the world, and win medals in jiu-jitsu, and he was looking for a book to help him turn these big goals into reality. Unfortunately, he hit a bit of a problem.

He looked in bookstores and searched online, but he couldn't find anything that gave him valuable insight into how to be the best he could possibly be. Nathan was faced with two choices: accept that there wasn't anything like this out there, or do something about it.

Later that summer, Nathan met Danielle Brown, a double Paralympic gold medallist and five-time World Champion in archery. Danielle is a public speaker and was talking about what it takes to become the best in the world. Nathan asked her whether she had written a book to help children become the best they could be. When she said no, he asked whether he could write one with her. And here it is.

Success doesn't happen by accident and it certainly doesn't happen overnight. Turning your life into a success is about committing to being focused, motivated, confident, and AWESOME. It's about working on all the different areas that make you the unique and perfect individual you are. And it's about sticking with it each and every day.

This book contains lots of techniques, tips, suggestions, and ideas for you to try out. It's a road map that points you in the right direction and takes you on a step-by-step journey to develop the skills that many successful people use to help them become fantastic at what they do.

Whenever you set out on a long journey, it is important to take the supplies that you need with you. Each chapter covers a different, but very important skill that you can use on your journey. We explain how this skill can help you and suggest things you can work on.

Please remember that this is your book and your journey to success, so take your time and go along at your own pace. You might find it helpful to work your way through this book with a trusted adult who can discuss some of the ideas with you and help you apply them to your daily life.

WHAT IS SUCCESS?

Do you want to be successful? Of course you do! When we achieve something, we feel really great about ourselves. In fact, there's no better feeling than succeeding, whether it's getting good grades, making it across the finish line, or feeling good about improving. Knowing that all your hard work has paid off is rewarding and makes you feel very proud. Knowing your worth is also massively important.

So you want to succeed, but what's the secret? How can you become the very best you can be? Our starting point is to try to define success.

SKILLS AND TALENTS

Success is difficult to describe because it is different for everybody. There's no one else out there quite like you! We are all good at something —in fact you are probably great at more than just one thing. We all have our own special set of skills, talents, and abilities, and we all have different hopes and dreams for the future too. The world would be a very boring place if everybody wanted to become a teacher, scientist, or athlete.

MEASURING SUCCESS

We measure success differently as well. For some people it means getting a good education and pursuing a dream career.

Success could also be traveling the globe, having a family, happiness, or making a difference in other people's lives. For a few people, it is achieving a challenging goal, or being the best in their club, school, country, or the world at a particular activity. Others measure it by the things they own, such as a big house or a fast car.

There are millions of different ways to be successful. Success could be anything, and how YOU define it might be completely different from what your friends think success looks like. It's important to start thinking about your own definition and the path you will take to achieve it.

Whatever your definition of success, it's all about being your TRUE self. Be authentic and honest and know that you are awesome.

NATHAN SAYS...
Success to me is knowing that I've met my goals and I can look back and see what I've achieved. Money would be nice, but I think it's more about actions and achievements and how I feel inside before, during, and after it all—because our path to growth and success never really stops.

Don't worry if you're really struggling to come up with a definition for success. It may take time.

SUCCESS FOR YOU

If success is different for everyone, then how do you know what success looks like for you? First, find the nearest mirror and take a look at your reflection. You are a success story waiting to happen. You have all the tools, abilities, and talents that you will ever need to help you achieve your own definition of success.

Now, see if you can get a glimpse of the future you. Try to picture what you might look like when you have reached success and become the best version of yourself you can possibly be.

You have brains in your head. You have feet in your shoes. You can steer yourself any direction you choose.

DR. SEUSS, FROM
OH, THE PLACES YOU'LL GO!

Be your best self

10

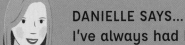

DANIELLE SAYS...
I've always had big plans for my future. I knew I wanted to be successful, but I found it difficult to decide how. I've wanted to be a doctor, a vet, a lawyer, a businesswoman, and an author. I kept changing my mind and couldn't decide what would make me happiest. I never even considered sports as a career until I was a teenager. Even when I haven't known exactly what I wanted from life, two things have always stayed the same:
- I have always chosen to pursue goals that excite me.
- I use the same tools to achieve success in my sport, education, and career.

VISUALIZING YOUR FUTURE

Imagining or picturing a successful you is a great place to start. This is called VISUALIZATION. When you visualize yourself in the future, you make it more likely to happen. When we see ourselves achieving goals, we start to believe that it is possible.

Don't worry if visualization doesn't come naturally to you. It's something we can all learn to do with practice.

If you don't know what your success story looks like, it's alright. Nathan spent a long time thinking about his definition of success and he hasn't narrowed it down to just one specific career or life goal. For him,

success is about feeling satisfied, happy, proud, and great about who he is and what he has achieved.

So don't worry if you aren't certain about what you want from your future. This book is here to help you answer these questions. What we can say is that if you are working on becoming the best version of yourself, and the things that make you who you are, you will find the path to success much easier.

Who knows what opportunities will land on your doorstep? You might find something that you hadn't even thought of. The skills in this book can help you make the most of it.

DREAM BIG

Has anybody ever told you to follow your dreams? This is great advice. You see, there are no shortcuts to success. If you want to be good at anything, you have to work hard to get there. No ifs, no buts, no excuses.

If you're really passionate about something then you'll WANT to put time and effort into becoming really good at it. You'll be eager to work through the challenges and the boring parts that pop up on your journey. When you're thinking about future achievements and successes it's important to DREAM BIG.

Success doesn't happen by accident. If you want to be good at something, you have to work for it.

EXCITING DREAMS

Success starts with a dream—a tiny idea that blossoms into something magnificent. Dreams don't have to be limiting. They should be big and exciting, and perhaps even a little bit scary. If your dream goal excites you enough, then it will fill you with the energy to keep going. It makes you push yourself harder and further than you ever thought was possible.

You might not reach that dream in a few months or even years, but if your dream burns strong enough and long enough, if you dedicate enough of your time and effort to it, then you will get closer and closer. Even if you never hit the mark or eventually decide that it's not the right thing, you will learn a lot from trying.

Never give up on what you really want to do. The person with big dreams is more powerful than the one with all the facts.

ALBERT EINSTEIN

DANIELLE SAYS...
A year after I started archery I was invited to help out at the Junior World Championships. When I saw the Great Britain team in their red tracksuits, a shiver ran down my spine. I wanted one of those tracksuits. I wanted to represent my country, and I told myself that was what I was going to do.

It was a HUGE dream. Being the best in your country at something is no easy task, but I was determined. I worked hard, even on the days when I was tired and would have preferred to be at home. I went out to train in the cold and rain. I got up early, so I could fit my practice around schoolwork. Two years later I got my Great Britain tracksuit, and I was so proud of that achievement!

Be your best self

Setting yourself a big, exciting, scary goal is really motivating and encourages you to keep going, even through setbacks.

WHAT ARE YOU PASSIONATE ABOUT?

Having a BIG dream increases your motivation and commitment to achieving it. You might not be sure what your dream looks like at the moment. One way to figure this out is to look at yourself as a whole person and answer these three questions:

What are you really passionate about?
What drives you to take action?
What are your strengths?

When thinking about this, you should be looking a bit deeper than simply what you like or dislike. Being passionate means you're so enthusiastic about something that you spend a lot of time thinking about it and make time to do it. It's not something you do just for fun. As well as looking at your passions, look at your strengths and your motivations—the reasons why you want to do this.

BIG GOALS

Setting yourself a big goal at this stage is a much better idea than having small goals that you can achieve easily. If your sights are set too low, then you don't push yourself towards achieving your potential.

Some people can be a little bit worried about setting gigantic goals though. They think "I'd love to achieve that, but I'll never be good enough." If something like this has ever crossed your mind then you will find the chapter on self-confidence useful. It will teach you how to ignore this unhelpful little voice and allow you to start thinking big, because you ARE capable of brilliance if you put your mind to it.

VISION BOARD

Once you've thought up your dream goal, draw a picture of it or find photos that show it and create a poster. This is called a VISION BOARD. Display it where you can see it every day, and it will spur you on, reminding you what you're working for.

When thinking about your dream goal, look at your passions, your strengths, and your motivations to achieve it.

GOAL SETTING

Once you have got an idea about what you want to achieve, the next step is to figure out how to do it. Luckily, there is a really useful tool that can help you with all this. Yes, you've guessed it—goal setting.

If you don't have a plan, it's like deciding to travel across the country without a map, compass, or GPS. You're likely to become lost or end up going around in circles. Like a map, goal setting helps you reach your destination.

Great things are done by a series of small things brought together.

VINCENT VAN GOGH

Goal setting is our road map to get to where we want to go.

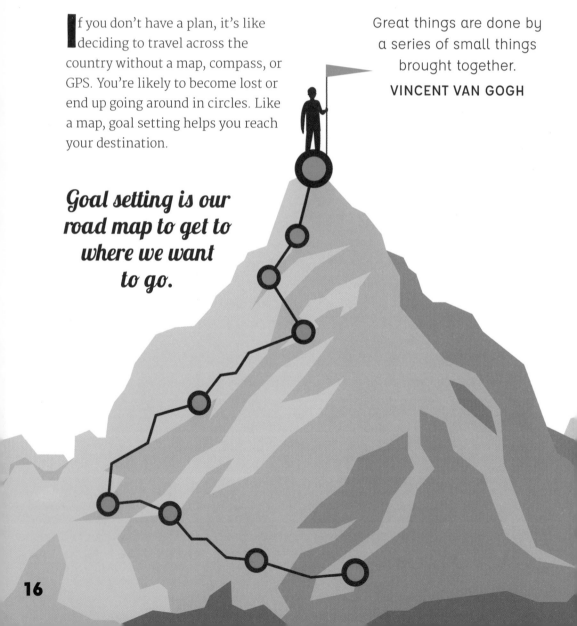

When you achieve short-term goals on the journey to the big goal, your self-confidence gets a boost.

Goal setting helps you to come up with a clear plan. It motivates you to keep going, inspiring you to work hard to reach your goals. Goal setting can help you to make big decisions, giving you the confidence that you are making the right choices. And once you know what you want to achieve, you can let your support team know so your family and friends can help you.

Danielle didn't have much luck with goal setting to start with because she was not taught how to do it properly. Because of this, her training was a bit like playing a game of snakes and ladders. She would make progress and take a few steps forward, only to find herself slipping back down a snake a few moves later. That's why it is important to make time for goal setting.

DANIELLE SAYS...
I thought goal setting was a waste of time before learning how to do it properly. I knew what I wanted—to win every gold medal I could get my hands on! I couldn't see how sitting down and writing about it was going to help. But I couldn't have been more wrong. It might not be the most exciting thing to do, but setting goals increases the chance of you achieving them. Coming up with a clear plan meant that I knew exactly what I had to work on to keep improving, and I started to win more and more medals. Goal setting really helped me to stay focused and I progressed much more quickly than I had done before.

All you can do in life is follow your dreams. Otherwise you're just wasting your time.

DAVID WALLIAMS

STEPLADDER TO SUCCESS

In the last section, you looked at your BIG dream goal. Now, let's start working on making it come true. It's all very well and good if you know where you want to go. But it won't do you much good if you don't know how you're going to get there.

This is the part where we create a plan and break down that super-exciting, stupendously big goal into smaller chunks. This is where we build a stepladder to success.

If you've only ever swum a couple of lengths and you decide that you want to swim the Channel to France, this isn't something you will manage in the space of a week. It's going to take training, building yourself up so you're strong enough, and developing a good swimming technique. You will need a good plan to tackle that challenge.

SMALL STAGES

Whenever we travel somewhere new, directions come in handy. Your stepladder to success helps you to create a road map that will help you get there. Your stepladder is made up of short-term targets that break the big goal down into smaller stages that are easier to achieve. While the aim is to reach your dream goal, there's no reason that you can't enjoy the journey.

Each rung you climb is a cause for celebration. Celebrating success helps us realize that what we are doing is worthwhile. It's motivates and refreshes us before we look toward the next rung on the ladder and repeat the process. And it's great to feel that you are paving the way to achieving your long-term goal.

So how do you do it?

Think about the first rung on your stepladder and the actions you can take to reach it.

Your stepladder

Draw a stepladder and write your dream goal right at the very top. Next, think about the separate steps that make up that big goal. Each rung on your ladder is a stage in the journey towards your goal.

Goal: Be a chef in a top restaurant

WORK HARD AND PROGRESS

APPLY FOR KITCHEN JOBS

START TRAINING TO BE A CHEF

VISIT RESTAURANTS AND READ ABOUT COOKING

FIND A JOB IN A RESTAURANT

TRY OUT DIFFERENT KINDS OF COOKING

LEARN TO COOK AT HOME

Be your best self

MAKING GOOD CHOICES

Putting effort into waiting for good things to happen can be hard work. Sometimes, it seems more appealing to choose the option where we get pleasure right now. This is called instant gratification. It gives us a short burst of enjoyment, but it doesn't last very long.

Instant gratification is not always a bad thing. There's nothing wrong with having a bit of time to yourself to enjoy a favorite snack or game. The problem with it is that it's all about short-term gains. It doesn't take those BIG plans into account. Sometimes, the actions we take for a quick nice feeling can harm those long-term plans.

Take the example of playing video games. Yes, it's lots of fun and it is fine in small amounts. But if you spend hours and hours playing them, it means you aren't working on reaching the first rung on your stepladder to success.

Good things come to those who __work__ for them.

DANIELLE SAYS...
As an athlete, whenever I made a decision, I always asked myself the question, "is this going to help me win the gold medal?" Going to bed late and eating the wrong foods were not going to help me win gold, so I wouldn't do them, even if I was tempted sometimes. My long-term goal of winning gold at a Paralympic Games was more powerful than any short-term enjoyment I would have gotten from other activities.

We need to learn how to balance instant gratification with hard work. Learning how to be patient and not giving in to instant gratification is an important part of becoming the best version of yourself.

So how do we do it?

PRACTICING PATIENCE

Patience is a skill that can be learned by changing how you think. Instead of getting frustrated when things take longer than you want them to, try to accept that good things take time. You can practice developing patience by taking some small steps.

Learning patience not only helps you to focus on your DREAM goal, but it also helps you to become a happier person. Here are a few suggestions:

If you feel frustrated and impatient, take a deep breath and ask yourself why you feel this way. What can you do to make it better?

Set yourself a timer for the task you need to do. When it goes off, you can take a break.

Finish your homework before going out to play.

Be your best self

STAY ON THE RIGHT PATH

Life is full of choices. Imagine that the path in front of you splits into two directions. One is wild and winding, and leads towards a mountain range. The other is straight, lined with freshly cut grass, and there's an ice-cream van on the corner.

At first glance, the straight road seems like the better option, doesn't it? But would you change your mind if you knew that the road stops just after the ice-cream van? The winding road over the mountains will take a lot longer and be really hard work, but on the other side of the mountains is something truly spectacular.

Always ask yourself which option is more likely to help you get to your goal. You can choose the easy short-term win or the more difficult route with HUGE rewards at the end. If you want to be the very best you can be, then it's got to be the second option. Even though the route is difficult, there may be good times. The mountain path may be beautiful and the view from the top will take your breath away.

NATHAN SAYS...
I am currently working on getting the balance right while I am writing this book. I like to play, but everyone needs to work if they want to be the best they can be. Without effort and dedication and determination, you will end up with a big broken plan, and nobody wants that!

VISUALIZATION CAN HELP

If you are still tempted by instant gratification, try VISUALIZATION (see page 11). Picture yourself achieving your goal and think how amazing you will feel when you've finally done it. Make the image in your mind as clear as you can, ramping up the color, sounds, and feelings until it's really strong.

Take a deep breath and picture the temptation in your mind. See yourself walk away from it. Each step feels better, as you leave behind the temptation in the distance. Now you're walking toward your goal, feeling stronger than ever before.

Visualizing yourself walking away from temptation and toward your goal can help you stay on the right track.

How did you find that? Visualization is an incredible tool. It allows you to believe that the end goal is far more important than a small win right now. This means you are more likely to stick with it. The great thing about visualization is that you can practice it anywhere. A few minutes here and there will help you achieve your goal.

Be your best self

23

THE MIND AND MINDSET

You don't come into the world with "engineer" or "writer" stamped on your forehead. It is up to you to decide what success means in your life. And to achieve it, you need the right mindset.

WHAT IS MINDSET?

Our mindset is our beliefs and the way we see the world, which shapes the way we think, feel and behave. Professor Carol Dweck is an expert in mindsets, and she talks about two types: fixed and growth mindsets. Let's take a look.

FIXED MINDSET

If you believe you are naturally talented at something (or not), you have a fixed mindset. You might think you're super at swimming or fantastic at French. You might also think that you are terrible at tennis, dreadful at dancing or that you suck at science.

Thinking this way is not helpful. If you believe that you're either naturally good or bad at an activity, there is no room for improvement. We know that hard work and effort are big parts of being the best you can be.

If you think you can't do something, then you are talking yourself into failure. If one of your friends said, "I'm rubbish at running", on sports day, do you think they will be feeling confident as they line up for the race? Of course they won't. They believe they are no good at running and it affects their behavior.

Negative thoughts and feelings can prevent us from achieving amazing things and prevent us from becoming the best we can be.

It's a simple formula.
THOUGHTS + FEELINGS = BEHAVIOR

NATHAN SAYS...
I used to struggle with my piano practice and I felt bored and frustrated. I wanted to be outside playing, so sometimes I gave up and walked off. After learning about different mindsets I realized I had a choice. I decided that if I felt like stopping, I would check in with myself and my goals. If I really needed a break I'd take it. But if I was just trying to avoid practice, this wasn't the best choice to make.

Be your best self

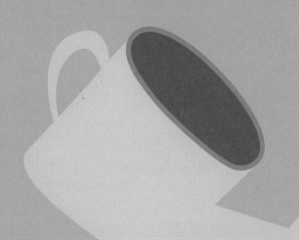

GROWTH MINDSET

If you have a growth mindset, you believe you can learn new skills. You focus on the areas you can control: your attitude, the amount of hard work you do, and how you respond to failure and bounce back from mistakes.

There's no limit to what you can learn!

A trip through the forest

Imagine an overgrown forest with vines and huge trees. You see long grass, mud, brambles, and roots everywhere. There is no path, and you have to turn back to find tools to cut through the brambles. You get scratched, trip up on hidden roots, and keep getting lost. You're scared that you will sink into a swamp. The journey feels overwhelming. But you keep going, and you find yourself enjoying it. Finally, you reach the other side, tired but happy.

The second time you go through the forest, you travel more quickly. It is still tricky, but you see the swamp and remember tripping over roots, so you don't walk that way again. You get dirty and sweaty, but you aren't quite so scared this time. You keep practicing, and it gets easier. In the end, you form a path through the forest.

PATHWAYS IN YOUR BRAIN

This is what happens in the brain every time you learn a new skill. At first, you have to concentrate hard. As you get better at it, you don't have to think so hard. This goes for anything you learn, whether it is math or playing an instrument.

The brain is like a muscle. The more you use it, the stronger it becomes. When you practice a skill or an action, it creates a pathway. If you repeat the action, the brain remembers and it becomes just a little bit easier each time.

DANIELLE SAYS...
When I first started archery I was TERRIBLE! I couldn't hit the target to save my life. I had to really concentrate. Over time, I didn't have to think so much about what I was doing because my brain knew what to do and I didn't make as many mistakes.

How can I get a growth mindset?

To achieve a growth mindset, we need to tackle those negative fixed-mindset thoughts that sometimes pop into our head.

Remember the friend who said: "I'm terrible at running"? If they had a growth mindset, they could say: "I'm going to practice my running and try my best to improve." Here are some other negative fixed-mindset examples and how to change them:

"I'm terrible at this" 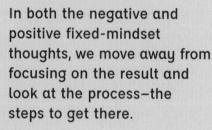 "I might not be great at it YET, but I'm working on getting better."

"This is way too hard for me" → "It's challenging, but if I approach it in the right way and work really hard, then I will get there."

"I know I'm going to fail, so there's no point in even trying" → "If I don't try, then I definitely will fail. If I give it a try, even if I fail, I can learn how to do better next time."

In both the negative and positive fixed-mindset thoughts, we move away from focusing on the result and look at the process—the steps to get there.

It's also important to change any positive fixed-mindset thoughts. They should focus on the actions we need to take to improve.

"I'm great at math" → "I've been working really hard at math recently and I'm doing better."

"This is good enough" → "I didn't give this work 100% and I know I can do better."

CHANGE YOUR MINDSET

Do you have any fixed-mindset thoughts about yourself? Write them down and see if you can come up with a growth-mindset idea instead.

Getting our mindset right is ESSENTIAL for success. Understanding the difference between growth and fixed mindsets is the first step of learning. When we learn more about the way we think, feel, and behave, we can make sure we are on the right track, or make changes if we need to.

Practice a growth mindset by seeing where you can improve and grow, how you can be more resilient, and finding new ways to get to your goal.

STAYING FOCUSED

Focus! Pay attention! Concentrate! How many times have you been told to do these things? These are all super-important things to be able to do. But has anybody ever told you why? When you focus, you get tasks done quickly and easily and you do them better, too.

I have always believed that if you want to achieve anything special in life you have to work, work, and then work some more.

DAVID BECKHAM

DISTRACTIONS

What can happen if you DON'T focus? Life can throw up a lot of distractions. A distraction is something that stops you from concentrating on what you're supposed to be doing. It could be a person rushing past or talking really loudly, or you can distract yourself. Do you ever sit down to do something but your mind wanders off and suddenly you're thinking about something else?

This is perfectly normal. Your brain doesn't come with an off switch. Thoughts are always popping into our mind, even if we are sitting in a nice, quiet space and intend to focus on a task. Perhaps we are thinking about what we're going to eat for lunch or where we're going for the weekend. We might feel bored or tired, or feel like watching videos instead. These are all distractions.

If you don't focus...

You waste a lot of time.

You might be distracted by an activity that gives you instant gratification. It feels good at the time, but it pulls you away from the activities that are important to you. Then you feel bad.

It can be dangerous. If you're not concentrating near a busy road, for example, you can put yourself in terrible danger.

NATHAN SAYS... This book has taken months of work. It has required a lot of FOCUS and avoiding distractions. Coming out of school and trying to write has been difficult at times. So what did I do?

First, I have my loved ones to thank for always encouraging me to keep going. Second, I used positive thoughts to help my writing flow when I got stuck.

Taking charge of your mind

The great news is that we can learn how to control our mind and become better at focusing on the tasks that will help us reach our goals. This is where WILLPOWER comes in. Being determined is vital in your journey to success. You need to accept that distractions happen. The key is learning how to bring yourself back to the task.

Here are some tips to help you deal with distractions:

1 Create a quiet environment where you have as few distractions as possible. Make sure you work away from your TV, tablet, or phone.

2 Keep your vision on your work. If you start to look around, this is a sign that you're being distracted and need to bring your focus back.

3 Say your goals out loud or to yourself. You could write them down on paper. Focus on ONE task at a time.

4 When you notice you've been distracted, bring yourself back by saying things like "This is what I am supposed to do. This is my work."

5 If you are finding it hard to concentrate on your work, ask a friend or family member for ideas on how to focus better.

6 Be forgiving if you keep getting distracted, and gently pull yourself back to the task. It can take time to learn to control your mind.

7 Let your brain have a break—it needs a rest after all that hard work! Give it a few moments to wander before returning to the task at hand.

Learning to focus allows us to perform much better at tasks and stops us from wasting time.

GETTING ORGANIZED

To get better at any skill, you have to put a lot of time and effort into it. While there aren't many shortcuts to success, there are often SMARTER ways to get there. Getting organized is one of them.

DISORGANIZED

If you're disorganized, you don't know where things are meant to be. Imagine you're going to a swimming lesson in 20 minutes and you can't find your gym bag. How much time do you spend rushing around the house, trying to remember where you saw it last? How worried do you feel when it's not where it's supposed to be?

When you finally realize that it somehow ended up in the closet under the stairs, you're ten minutes late for your class. This means that you're not going to be the very best you can be at swimming.

ORGANIZED

Some people say being organized is all about keeping a clean, tidy bedroom and a clear desk. This is true, but it's only part of being organized.

Being organized is a state of mind. It starts with how you think and plan. If you're organized, you put your things in the right place so you can find them later. You also know when your homework is due and get your bag ready the evening before. If you're organized, you can make the most of the time you've got.

DANIELLE SAYS... Being organized was never natural for me. I always had these great ideas in my head but I didn't think I had time to write them all down and come up with a proper plan. So I didn't. I realized that this was not the most effective use of my time. I started organizing myself and noticed I had more time on my hands.

Quicker to be messy?

You might think keeping your bedroom tidy takes up too much time. It's so much faster to throw your clothes on the floor rather than fold them up and put them away, isn't it?

Well actually... no! If you spend five minutes putting your clothes away, it will take up far less time than sorting out your entire wardrobe at the end of the week. And a clutter-free room makes a more relaxing and happier environment than a messy one.

Put things back in the right place when you've finished with them. It will make your life easier in the long run.

BECOMING WELL ORGANIZED

Getting organized is about forming good habits. At first, you might find it hard to keep your room tidy. But once you are used to it, you will wonder how you managed any other way! And if you think you're bad at it, remember that with a growth mindset, any skill can be learned. You can become much better at being organized if you practice.

NATHAN SAYS...
My brother and I used to leave our clothes all over the bedroom floor. It was difficult to find what we wanted, and all of our clothes got wrinkled. Now we always put them away. I love taking care of my clothes, and a tidy room feels much better to be in!

TO DO LISTS

A good way to get organized is to write a To Do list. If you write down all your tasks for the week, you'll have a good plan. You can organize your time to fit everything in. The list helps you stay organized and focus on the things you need to do to achieve your big goals.

The best thing about a To Do list is crossing off the items when you've completed them, which makes you feel AWESOME! Seeing everything you have done gives you a feeling of satisfaction, which motivates you to keep going.

PREPARATION

Let's take a look at preparation. When opportunities come knocking on your door, you need to be ready for them.

Think about chess players: they wouldn't enter a competition without training for it really hard. They would make sure to rest, eat, and drink beforehand. And they would show up in plenty of time so they're in the best place mentally before their event. Otherwise, they might feel nervous and under-confident.

If we write things down, we are more likely to carry them out.

The Three Ps

Plan
Come up with a plan for when you are going to practice and pack. Figure out when you need to be ready and what time you will need to leave. If you have a good plan, you will feel less stressed.

Practice
If you want to get better at any skill, you need to practice it. The more prepared you are, the better chance you have of success.

Pack
Make sure you have everything you need before you go. It might be easiest to do this the night before.

Be your best self

HOW TO KEEP GOING WHEN THE GOING GETS TOUGH

Sometimes things don't go according to plan. It can feel difficult when this happens. We may feel disappointed, or helpless about things that are out of our control. Even when things don't go wrong, sometimes we just feel tired or unmotivated. What do we do then?

RESILIENT MINDSET

Resilience is a skill that helps us to bounce back when things go badly. It allows us to be strong inside, hold our head high, and try again.

The first step to building a resilient mindset is to understand that these times will happen. When we accept this, we can put plans in place so we can keep going when the going gets tough.

If you're losing your mojo, it can be helpful to remind yourself of your goals and list all the reasons you want to achieve them. This is an opportunity to rekindle the drive that set you off on that journey.

MAKE NEGATIVE COMMENTS POSITIVE

Negative attitudes and comments from others can bring us down. But instead of believing them, we can change them into positive ideas. For example, you can turn "You'll never be able to do that!" into "I'll prove you wrong and show you I can do it."

Turning around negative thoughts helps us to focus on the steps we can take to improve.

Remembering why you want to achieve your goals will help motivate you when life gets tough.

LEARN FROM MISTAKES

If you know that it is OK to make mistakes, it will help you to keep going. People often think that mistakes are a bad thing, but this is not true. Mistakes are actually incredibly important because you can learn from them.

Try to accept the disappointed feelings, but instead of fretting, use a growth mindset to get over the problem. Think about what didn't work this time around and try something else. Look for helpers who might see the problem with different eyes and find a solution. If you need more help, ask an expert who knows more about your goals or do some research yourself. You might need to use a different method, but keep at it and stay determined.

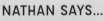

NATHAN SAYS...
I have experienced some people being unkind to me and even trying to make things go wrong. I felt very upset that they didn't understand me or my good intentions. But I learned that I need to rely on myself, the positive messages and the good people around me. I don't let others spoil my plans.

Be your best self

CONTROLLING YOUR RESPONSE

Often when the going gets tough, it's because of things out of our control. This can make us feel frustrated, worried, or stressed. If we put all our energy into worrying and feeling down, we are not helping ourselves to become the best we can be.

We want to let you into a secret. There are lots of things that you can't control: the weather, moving to a new school, or other people's opinions of you. But there is one thing that you do have control over: YOURSELF!

You have control over YOURSELF!

You can control your ATTITUDE —how often you smile and how kindly you speak to yourself and others. It's up to you whether you ask for help and how much effort you put into your projects. You are in control of how much time you (don't!) spend fretting!

Although you might not be able to control the situation, you can control your RESPONSE to it. When something bad happens, take a nice deep breath. Ask yourself what is the best way to respond to the situation. Can you change something you're doing to make it better?

It is healthy to acknowledge your feelings, but remember that you control them, they don't control you. Affirm to yourself: "I can handle this. I can do this."

Instead of disappointment taking over, put your focus and energy back on where it needs to be—on becoming the best you can be! This is the beautiful growth mindset at work.

Always keep focused on the things you can control.

LEARNING HOW TO FAIL WELL

Why is there a chapter about failing in a book about success? That's a great question. How you deal with failure is vital if you want to succeed.

Here's another question for you to think about. Do you think lightbulbs are a good invention? We can almost hear you say, "Yes! Of course!" They're a big improvement over reading by candlelight, right?

Did you know that Thomas Edison failed more than 10,000 times when he tried to invent the lightbulb? Yet he kept on going and was determined to succeed. Eventually, he created a lightbulb that worked.

> We speak about success all the time. It is the ability to resist failure that often leads to greater success.
>
> **J. K. ROWLING**

Failure happens to everybody, so we need to learn how to manage it properly.

Failure can teach us so much. Keep focused on the lessons it brings.

A CHANCE TO LEARN

The greatest winners in life weren't always at the top of their game. They made mistakes, faced challenges, and failed.

Instead of being knocked off course every time they had a setback, they carried on. They saw the setback as experience—a chance to learn and get better. And they didn't give up their dreams.

It feels horrible if you lose or do badly in a test. You might be frustrated, angry, or disappointed. Managing to cope with these emotions is an important skill. Failure does not mean that you can't do something. It means that you can't do it yet, or you have to find a different way to achieve it. You need to look at the situation as positively as you can.

DANIELLE SAYS...
I failed at my first international event. I was so nervous that I started shaking. After allowing myself a little time to calm down, I looked at my performance and asked where it had gone wrong. I was nervous, I wasn't focused properly, and I thought it would be easy. These were all things I could work on to improve. I used my failure as fuel to motivate myself to practice harder, and a year later I went to the World Championships. I broke eight World Records in a week and won two gold medals.

Be your best self

WHENEVER YOU LOSE, YOU LEARN

Your journey to success will probably involve losing at some point. When this happens, you have two options.

1 You can accept failure.

2 You can take a deep breath, examine the situation, learn what went wrong, and adjust your strategy. Leave that failure behind and look for another way to get the results you want.

WHICH OPTION WOULD YOU CHOOSE?

Of course, option 2 is a much better choice. Each time you do this, you become more resilient. When we fail, it is super important to adopt a resilient mindset:

Don't get discouraged or give up.

Remember that successful people are persistent— they continue to work towards their goal.

Use failure as a motivation to do better next time.

MOTIVATION

Motivation keeps popping up through this book because it's a key skill in becoming the best version of yourself. When life throws challenges your way, it's important to understand what drives you to keep going. On the toughest days, you're going to need to hold on to this thought.

If you have made a mistake or have failed at something and are feeling discouraged, please remember: Persistence and resilience are the qualities of successful people. If you keep on trying, you'll succeed.

If you need to change your tactic after things have gone wrong, then you will get closer and closer to success. You __are__ becoming the best version of yourself.

NATHAN SAYS...
My first jiu-jitsu competition was the European Championships. I was prepared in technique, but not for the speed or hunger of my competitors. I got floored with an awesome takedown in the first few seconds.

My next competition was The King Of The North. I was prepared for speed and had humongous hunger, but I was not prepared to fight somebody way heavier and larger than me and I was beaten. I was devastated. I'd done everything and I thought I had it, but that was a fixed mindset!

I talked with my mom and knew that these results were going to change, because my mindset changed. I learned how to compose my emotions and manage defeat. You either win or LEARN, and each fight was a learning experience. Using a growth mindset helped me realize that medals would follow.

Do you know what happened next? I fought in the National Championships—I won my fight, but lost the next and took home a bronze medal!

YOU ARE UNIQUE

What does it mean to be unique? It means that you're special—one of a kind. Everybody has their own strengths, talents, dreams for the future, unique thoughts, and their own unique weaknesses.

It's really important to embrace your uniqueness and enjoy being YOU. Stand up for what you believe in and stay true to yourself. Copying what everybody else is doing won't help you on your own journey to success and become the best, authentic, most amazing you!

PEER PRESSURE

When you're growing up though, there can be quite a lot of pressure to fit in with your peers. We all want to be liked, accepted, and respected. Many people feel that to get positive reactions from others, they should act and behave like everybody else. This is not true.

I don't want other people to decide who I am.
I want to decide that for myself.
EMMA WATSON

If you can relate to this, that's okay – it's perfectly normal to feel this way.

Following the crowd will NOT help you to become the best version of yourself. Learning about yourself and loving the things that make you special will boost your long-term happiness, even if it means splitting off from your friends every now and again. Once you stop trying to fit in and start being yourself, you will find a space where you truly belong.

DANIELLE SAYS... We all have likes and dislikes and these can often be different from other people's. We get along with some people beautifully and we might not gel with others. This is fine—the important thing is finding a group of people who will support and love you for who you are.

You are unique and you are awesome. Celebrate it!

SELF-AWARENESS

Let's have a little look at how well you know yourself.

This is called SELF-AWARENESS. If you're self-aware, you know who you are, where you want to go and what you want to do with your life. You also understand what's important to you.

Other things to consider are:

- what you like to eat
- what and who you like to play with
- what you're good at
- how you feel
- what you don't like
- what you're worth (clue: A LOT)

WHAT MAKES YOU SPECIAL?

To help you learn more about yourself, draw pictures or write down what makes you unique.

Knowing yourself is a valuable tool. Without self-awareness, setting goals and becoming the best you can be is going to be difficult. Listen to yourself and what you really want. Find out what you're good at, and what you're not so good at right now. When it comes to getting to know yourself, all information is useful.

Try to spend time with people who will help you to become the real you, not a version of yourself that you think somebody else wants. If you can't be yourself, it will be difficult to feel truly happy.

NATHAN SAYS...
Yoga has really helped me understand myself better. It has helped me to become aware of my own body and what it can or cannot do, how it wants to move, and whether it's fidgety or not.

Yoga also helps me with my feelings because when you're sad it can make you happy, and when you're angry or fidgety, it can make you calm and still.

Self-awareness is key to developing healthy self-esteem, self-love, and self-confidence. Confidence comes from within you, from knowing, accepting, and liking who you are.

SELF-CONFIDENCE: THE KEY TO SUCCESS

What do you think self-confidence is? Well, it's not something you can touch, taste, or buy. Self-confidence is belief in your own ability to do things and be successful.

BELIEVE IN YOURSELF

Even if you can't do the thing you want to do at this exact moment, if you're self-confident, you know that you will get there in the end. It's learning what you need, knowing what you're capable of, and acting in a way that shows it.

PERSON 1

'I can't do it—this is too hard.'

'I'm not smart enough.'

'Everyone thinks I'm dumb.'

'I don't like myself.'

'I'm worthless, so I may as well give up now.'

PERSON 1 is cruel to themselves, and this won't have a positive effect on their confidence.

PERSON 2 has a positive outlook and speaks to themself like their own best friend.

Self-confidence is the key to success, and the best news is that it doesn't happen by chance. You can learn it! You CAN create the life you want.

One way to tell if you're feeling confident or not is by listening to the things you tell yourself. Use positive messages when talking to yourself, and believe that you ARE capable, and you CAN do it—even if it feels hard.

What does your voice say when you're talking to yourself? Can you improve on it to make you feel more confident? If you want to be more confident, start saying good things to yourself.

If you notice yourself saying negative, hurtful things, take a deep breath, give yourself a hug on the inside and focus on positive, powerful things.

Self-confidence is a skill you need to keep working on to be the best you can be—to stand out from the crowd and shine.

Self-confidence comes from knowing you can do something, and once you've done it—even if you didn't feel super confident—then you've learned that you are capable of doing it. You did it. Hold on to that feeling!

You're braver than you believe, and stronger than you seem, and smarter than you think.

A.A. MILNE/CHRISTOPHER ROBIN

Building your self-confidence

Self-confidence can be learned with practice.
Here are some steps you can take.

- Pay attention to your posture. Try to stand tall, with your head held high and a confident expression on your face.
- Think about your behavior. Make sure you look as if you are in control of yourself.

- Keep clean and dress nicely. If you look confident on the outside, it helps you to feel confident on the inside.
- See if you can speak in a clear voice, and don't speak too quietly.

FAKE IT!

If you're feeling a little unsure, it helps to pretend to be more confident. It might feel false to start with, but over time, it actually turns into genuine confidence.

You can learn, fake, and create confidence.

When you can, SMILE! Our facial expressions don't just show what a person is feeling. They create that feeling. When you smile even if you don't feel like it, your mood can improve. (Creating feelings also happens if you frown. If you fake a frown it can make you feel grumpy, tense or unhappy.) Smiling, even when you are a bit nervous, can create good, confident feelings.

USE VISUALIZATION

You can use visualization in any situation where you feel a little unconfident (see page 11). Want to become better at making friends? Picture yourself confidently approaching somebody new and asking how they are. The more we practice this, the more confident we will become.

Now imagine your future self, reaching your dream goal. See, hear, feel, smell, and taste your achievement. Picture the other people around you—how might they act? Imagine how confident you will be when all that hard work has paid off, and you have become the best you can be.

WALL OF SUCCESS

To feel more confident, try to focus on the positive and celebrate your successes. It's good to remember your achievements and reflect on what you did well. When other people notice you've done well and give you compliments, it's important to accept and remember them too.

Writing down your achievements before you forget them can be helpful —you can look over them if you ever feel like you need a confidence boost. If you're really struggling to find any achievements, ask a friend or adult if they can help you spot them!

You might also like to create a Wall of Success on a bulletin board where you will see it every day. This is a powerful tool. Stick up positive thoughts and photos of your main achievements. Every time you see your wall, you are reminded that you can—and do—achieve great things.

COPING WITH UNDER-CONFIDENCE

When we're nervous, our brain sometimes plays tricks on us and blows things out of proportion. If you feel nervous or unsure, pay attention to what's going on. Does your tummy feel jittery? Do your hands feel restless? Is your heart beating too fast?

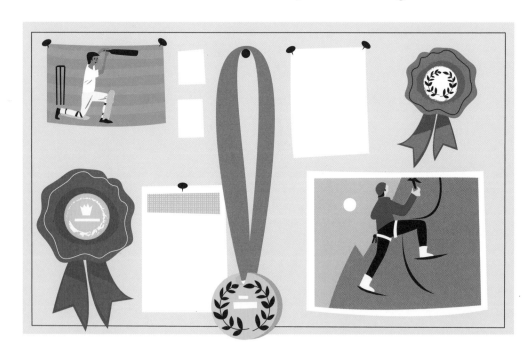

Dealing with nerves

When we're nervous, our brain sometimes plays tricks on us and blows things out of proportion. If this happens to you, ask yourself:

1 Is my life in immediate danger?

2 If it goes wrong, will it affect the work I have done?

3 Do I really have a reason to be nervous?

A lot of the time, the answer to these questions will be a big "NO!" So you can let go of these feelings. If the answer is "yes", speak to a trusted adult immediately.

Look at the situation and focus on controlling your response (see page 40). Tell yourself something positive, such as "It's OK. I will breathe deeply and count to ten, telling myself positive messages about myself, and then I will feel calmer."

Once you realize things are alright and you have controlled your response, you will feel more confident, brave, and resilient. Go you!

Practice and succeed at small things, such as getting your first medal at gymnastics. These small wins will pave the way to bigger successes, and you will feel better and better about yourself.

Lots of small wins add up to big ones.

PHYSICAL CHECK-IN

Everybody has physical needs every hour of every day. These include food, water, and sleep, and it is very important to meet them. Not meeting them can make us feel uncomfortable and cause problems.

Have you ever been scolded for not sitting still? Perhaps you needed to pee but were too focused on what you were doing to go to the restroom. If you have physical needs, it can be hard to listen or behave well, let alone shine and be the best you can be.

If you don't take care of your body, it can affect your confidence. It is difficult to perform at the best of your ability when you don't feel comfortable.

Worse still, if you're not taking care of your physical needs, then you're not properly taking care of yourself, and that is a sad thought.

You deserve only the best care, which includes taking care of yourself. There's no shame in politely excusing yourself for two minutes if you need to. In fact, doing that makes you AWESOME at taking care of yourself.

How to meet your needs

If your needs aren't met, it can be a huge barrier to being the best you can be. It's important to be aware of your body. Check in with yourself as you go through the day, and ask yourself:

- **Do I need to eat something?**
- **Do I need a drink?**
- **Do I need the toilet?**
- **Am I too hot?**

- **Am I too cold?**
- **Am I tired and need a rest?**
- **Have I been sitting for too long and need some exercise?**

THE BIG ONE: SELF-ESTEEM

Self-esteem is quite different from self-confidence. We know that self-confidence is how we feel about our abilities. Self-esteem is how we think and feel about ourselves. Having high self-esteem means you value yourself and know you deserve the good things in life.

Somebody may seem like the most confident person on the outside, but they might have low self-esteem if they secretly feel bad about themselves on the inside.

If this sounds like you, don't worry. You can work on developing your self-esteem.

Try saying this out loud:

**I am worthy.
I am important.
I deserve my best.**

Keep saying it to yourself every day —because it's true.

Be your best self

58

How to build high self-esteem:

Physical needs

- Make sure that you keep active and exercise. Eat well and ensure you have enough rest and sleep—you are important, and deserve to look after yourself.

Be kind to yourself

- Know that you are important and lovable.
- Do something you enjoy every day.
- Think kind thoughts about yourself.

- Spend some "me time" alone.
- Realize that you matter. You make the world a better place just by being in it.

Choose your companions

- Figure out which people in your life make you feel good. Try to be around people who make you feel good and stay away from negative people who make you feel bad.
- Stay true to your values. Stick up for yourself and what you believe in.

IMPROVE YOUR SELF-ESTEEM

There are ways to raise your self-esteem. Focus on the great things about yourself. Write down at least 10 things that are great about you. If this is difficult, you could ask your family, friends or a teacher to help you. Look at one of your goals and imagine yourself trying to achieve it. What if a challenge or fear springs up? Can you imagine what you would do to solve it? Draw or write down the problem, or act it out. Now imagine yourself trying to overcome it.

People with high self-esteem know they can solve problems, are lovable, valuable, important, and worthy. Remember: you deserve to succeed and you are capable of achieving your goals, no matter how many difficulties may come your way.

Your self-worth is determined by you. You don't have to depend on someone telling you who you are.
BEYONCÉ

Be your best self

BE YOUR OWN BEST FRIEND

There is a saying, "if you make friends with yourself you will never be alone." If you speak to yourself as a best friend, you will be your biggest support team and you'll always guide yourself through.

When you're your own best friend, you can comfort yourself and know that you're still awesome no matter what happens. You can be your own support network when times are tough—and your own number-one fan.

NATHAN SAYS...
Sometimes I find it difficult to get to sleep, especially if I'm excited about something. But when I get tired I can get very emotional and sensitive. I know that if I'm being my own best friend, I should be kind to myself and get the sleep I need. I have learned that my physical needs are important so that I can be in top form.

A KIND FRIEND

Would you be unkind to your best friend? Would you tell them that they couldn't achieve their dream goal? That they weren't good enough, or smart enough or fast enough? Would you tell them that they weren't important?

Of course you wouldn't! You would be KIND to them. A good friend would be supportive and encourage them to do their very best. A good friend would try to cheer them up if they felt down and help them to achieve their goals.

This means that you have to treat YOURSELF the same way. You should always be kind to yourself.

Be your own biggest cheerleader–it's not big-headed, it's necessary!

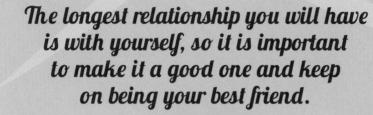

The longest relationship you will have is with yourself, so it is important to make it a good one and keep on being your best friend.

LOOKING AFTER YOURSELF

To be your own best friend, start by checking in with yourself. You can ask yourself questions like: How do I feel? Does that feel right? Is there anything I can do to make sure I have what I need? Meeting your physical needs is important—see page 56.

Emotional needs are vital too—taking care of our feelings. When we feel sad, it sometimes helps if family members or friends cheer us up, but it's REALLY important to learn to give good words of encouragement to ourselves.

It's also important to praise yourself if you have done something well. Recognizing your achievements helps you to focus your attention on the good stuff. Maintaining a positive attitude is a big part of becoming your best self.

You were made to be awesome—and you are!

You have to believe in yourself when no one else does.
SERENA WILLIAMS

DANIELLE SAYS...
A technique I use a lot is POSITIVE AFFIRMATIONS. These are positive statements that you say to yourself over and over again to help you build up belief in yourself. You can either say them out loud or silently in your head. They fill you with confidence and positivity. Affirmations are a fantastic way to deal with some of the negative thoughts that pop into your head every now and then.

One of my favorites is to tell myself "I've got this" when I'm in a situation that I'm unsure of and want to do my very best.

I am good enough.

TAKING ON NEW CHALLENGES

Your comfort zone is a space where you feel safe and secure. You become relaxed with routine and things that are familiar to you. In your comfort zone, life feels easy and comfortable.

The problem with comfort zones is that they do not allow us to grow and learn new things. They do not let us develop into our best self. When we step out of it, we have the chance to experience new opportunities and develop skills. Sometimes this can feel a little bit scary. But it's OK.

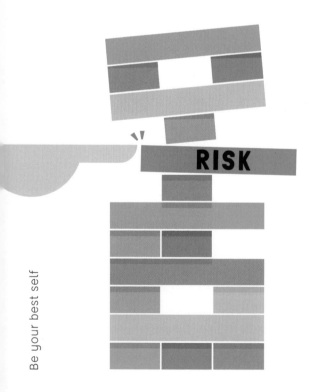

RISK

TAKING RISKS

If you were asked to take a pencil and draw, that would be very easy, right? But what if you were asked to look into a mirror and draw everything just by looking at the reflection? If you've never done this before, it could be difficult. Would you worry that you would scribble everywhere and your drawing wouldn't be any good? Or would you look forward to the challenge?

You see, leaving our comfort zone is a bit of a risk. Fantastic things might happen, or it could all go wrong. Some people find this exciting and leap right into it, but others may avoid trying new things because they are worried about failing.

In the section on learning how to fail well (see page 42), we learned that failure is good when we learn from the experience. So if getting out of your comfort zone—and even failure—are good things, what are you waiting for?

Be your best self

When you try something new and keep working at it, you learn a new skill, and over time you develop confidence. The more your confidence grows, the easier it becomes to try new things.

DANIELLE SAYS...

When I was at school I didn't like to put my hand up and ask questions. I was worried about looking silly in front of the rest of my class, so I kept my head down and my mouth closed. This wasn't helpful, because by keeping quiet I wasn't learning as much as I could.

When I finally asked a question it wasn't so bad. Nobody laughed. In fact, the teacher gave me some great feedback, which really helped. The first time I did this, it felt really scary. The second time, it wasn't so bad. Eventually, I wondered what I'd been worrying about in the first place—I learned much more and it helped other people too!

Take every chance you get in life. Because some things only happen once.

BEAR GRYLLS

HOW TO LEAVE YOUR COMFORT ZONE

Remember the growth mindset? We can learn any skill if we practice it. This means we can deal with anything outside our comfort zone. Here are some ideas how to do it.

1 TRY NEW THINGS

Say "yes" to an opportunity for a new experience. You can learn along the way, picking up the skills you need to be successful at it. And who knows? You might turn out to be extraordinarily good at it!

2 TAKE SMALL STEPS

If your goal was to climb up Mount Everest, you wouldn't just pull on your hiking boots and woolly hat and set off to the Himalayas. It's best to break your goal down into smaller steps (see page 18). First, you'd build up your strength and stamina. Then you'd climb small mountains, then higher ones, each one pushing you a little further until you are ready to reach the top of Everest.

NATHAN SAYS...
When I was learning to swim, I was scared of swimming to the deep end. I worried that there were sharks and octopuses that might eat me, even though I know they live only in saltwater. One day, I jumped straight in the deep end. This felt easier for me than swimming to the deep end from the shallow end.

I soon realized there were other people there who weren't being eaten by scary creatures. Once I had jumped in at the deep end and swum to the shallow end 20 times (out of my comfort zone), I realized I could swim to the deep end and back over and over again. Now I'm fearless and I love pounding out those laps!

3 BE FEARLESS

If you are worried about doing something challenging, then ask yourself what you are worried about. Sometimes our minds turn a small worry into a much bigger problem than it actually is.

Become FEARLESS by thinking of actions you can take to reduce your fear. With a solid plan, you will feel more comfortable.

4 USE POSITIVE TALK

Instead of worrying about failure, try to see it as an opportunity. Tell yourself that you CAN do it and then look for a way to get there.

BULLYING: STAY SAFE AND BE HEARD

Bullying might be familiar to some of you reading this book. We are sorry if this has happened to you. If you are bullied, it is extremely upsetting and it can knock your self-confidence and self-esteem.

There are different types of bullying. They include:

- Name calling (verbal)
- Pushing (physical)
- Cyber (on phones, computers, or tablets).

WHY DO PEOPLE BULLY OTHERS?

People often bully others because they feel jealous of them or insecure about themselves. Bullies may have low self–esteem. They don't know how to feel good about themselves so they pick on other people to feel more powerful.

But bullies are less powerful than you because they do not have the same positive attitude, confidence, and "people skills" to be kind to others like you do.

HOW TO DEAL WITH BULLIES

Talk to people you trust. Be vocal and loud about it, and tell as many people as you can, such as your parents, teachers, and caregivers. Tell them as soon as you can. If the first person cannot help, try someone else.

It is a good idea to keep a log of things that happen. Write down when it happened (date and time) and who saw it. The log will be useful when sharing information with others.

Kindness can also be a good strategy. It's tough to bully someone who says nice things. Use this strategy wisely though. We're not advising you to let the bullies walk all over you. Try to stay sure of yourself. You are unique, important, and special. You deserve respect and kindness.

NATHAN SAYS...
My younger brother Simeon says:
When someone is mean you might not want to play with them or spend time together. Sometimes this can feel very lonely. You might feel different from other children, and think that people don't understand you or that you deserve more respect. If you feel like this you are not on your own. Lots of children feel this way. Being different is good. Everyone is a person and they have to be different, otherwise it would be boring. It's not your fault if you are getting bullied. You didn't ask for it and you don't deserve it.

Being bullied is not your fault. People usually try to bully others because they are insecure about themselves.

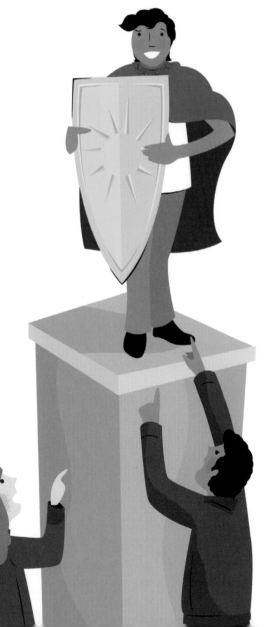

Be your best self

HOW TO STAY POSITIVE

Here are some tips to help you ignore negative comments so they don't affect you. It's called the STOP plan.

S Stay away—try to avoid being around the bullies as much as possible.

T Take care of yourself by spending time with other people so you don't have to cope alone.

O Open yourself to the power of positive self-talk. Remember to be your own best friend. Listen to yourself, like yourself, love yourself.

P Pictures—use visualization to make the bullies become smaller in your mind so that their comments don't affect you. You could imagine a cloak, shield, or force field that protects you from them. Think of a bouncy ball with their insults firing back at them or a firefighter's hose blasting the bullies so they are dripping wet.

A bully can only make you feel bad about yourself if you let them.

DAVID WALLIAMS

Never suffer in silence— find someone to talk to.

NATHAN SAYS... I'm naturally a gentle person. I was raised with a focus on talking through problems and thinking about others. When I went to school as a younger child, I got spat at, kicked, hit, and bullied. I didn't know what to do— this was a new and horrible world to me.

I realized that I needed to learn the skills to be able to defend myself in a confident and disciplined way. That was one of my reasons for starting jiu-jitsu —and at the age of eight I got bronze at the National Championships!

Stick up for yourself

Here are some top tips for stopping bullying:

- The bullies may ask you to do things that you think are wrong. Listen to your inner voice. Try to stand your ground and stay true to yourself and what you believe in. You don't need to give in to pressure. Although standing your ground takes bravery and confidence, you are worth it and you can do it.

- Make eye contact with the bully rather than looking away. If you find it difficult to look directly into another person's eyes, practice by looking at the color of a friend's eyes.

- Practice making brave and happy faces, and switch to "brave" mode if you're being bothered. How you look when you encounter a bully is even more important than what you say.

- Rehearse the right way to respond so you feel prepared. Speak in a strong, firm voice because whining or crying will only encourage a bully.

When someone is cruel or acts like a bully, you don't stoop to their level. No, our motto is, when they go low we go high.

MICHELLE OBAMA

Be your best self

IF YOU'VE BEEN CALLED A BULLY

If you have been wrongly accused of bullying, then speak to a trusted adult gently but firmly and explain your point of view.

Maybe it is true that you have acted like a bully, which might make you feel ashamed. If so, it is good that you realize your behavior was wrong. The first step in dealing with a problem is being aware of it. Do you feel that people don't understand you? Perhaps you're having problems managing your feelings. It's important to talk about this with someone you can trust. Remember: you are a worthwhile, deserving person.

By following the steps in this book you're already on your way to being the best you can be. Think about being your own best friend. If you're GENUINELY your own best friend and come from a place of kindness, there will never be any need to pull others down—you'll be bringing them upward with you!

DANIELLE SAYS...
I was bullied at school because I didn't fit in with most people. My clothes were different, my hair was frizzy, and I had different interests. I got called names and I was always the last to be picked for teams. It was upsetting and I wished I fitted in more.

I had a small group of close friends. This meant that I was around people who had similar interests as me, rather than people who had nothing helpful or kind to say. These friendships helped me to drown out the negative comments and feel better about myself.

Later, I realized that being popular is completely different from being successful. Being true to yourself, fighting for what you believe in, and sticking to your goals are more important. I also learned that the people you respect are those who really matter.

KINDNESS

You've probably been told hundreds of times that it's important to be kind to others. We're not going to tell you anything different—but we will explain why being kind helps you become the very best you can be.

When you are kind to others, it makes you feel great about yourself. When you feel good about yourself, it helps build your confidence and self-esteem. Kindness goes beyond this though. Not only does it make you feel good about yourself, it makes others feel good too. Being kind helps us to make new friends much more easily and strengthens the friendships that we already have.

A single act of kindness throws out roots in all directions,
and the roots spring up and make new trees.

AMELIA EARHART

DANIELLE SAYS...
Kindness was something I was taught when I was growing up. As I got older, people started to focus on other qualities such as ambition and determination. These are important, of course, but we should never forget how powerful being kind can be. I found that if you're kind to somebody, the returns you get are much greater. People are much more likely to help you if you're kind to them. It might not happen straight away, but over time it creates opportunities. Not only that, but it feels GREAT! There's nothing more rewarding than helping somebody succeed or knowing that you've cheered somebody up and brightened their day!

People will forget what you said.
People will forget what you did.
But people will never forget how
you made them feel.

MAYA ANGELOU

HOW TO BE KIND

Kindness starts with being thoughtful. It means taking time to think about how other people might feel in a certain situation. Once you understand how somebody is feeling, you can help them in the right way. If your friend gets some bad news, you can be there for them, offering a listening ear.

Being kind is about noticing when somebody needs help—you might open a door for them if they're carrying a heavy bag. Perhaps you can explain something to a friend that you picked up quite quickly but that they're struggling to understand.

NATHAN SAYS... To me, being kind means helping others, admiring what they do, listening very carefully, and not ignoring them. It can also be when you do a good deed for someone or have a friendly conversation, noticing good things about them.

If you're kind, you stand up for what is right and don't follow the crowd by spreading nasty gossip. You remember to ask after people, put effort into learning more about their lives and pay attention to what they have to say.

Kindness means expecting nothing in return. You are not being kind just to win approval from others, or to get stickers, points, and candy. The chances are that if you're kind, GREAT things will come your way. But that should not be your main reason for behaving with kindness.

CARE FOR YOURSELF TOO

Please remember that being kind doesn't mean that you have to say "yes" every time somebody asks you for a favor, or always put other people first. If you did this, you would never have time to work on becoming the absolute best you could be. If you've got far too many things on your "to do" list, it's OK to say that you can't help out this time. You can still be caring, respectful, and kind, but take care of yourself at the same time.

Of course, remember to be kind to yourself. Kindness really does start from within—you will find it much easier to be kind to others if you are kind to yourself.

If you're kind, good things may happen, but don't expect them to happen right away, or to be rewarded for your kindness all the time.

PEOPLE SKILLS

The world is filled with billions of people and to make our own mark on it, we need to learn how to get on with others. Having good people skills is a helpful and important part of being your best self.

Every part of life, from making friends to getting a good job and succeeding in life, requires good people skills. You might have fantastic strengths, but if you find it hard to get along with people, you will struggle to do well.

Just like any skill, people skills can be learned. Let's take a look at some ways to improve them.

Hello, nice to meet you.

Be polite and friendly

Good manners are important. They make the people you interact with feel valued, and if they feel valued, they are far more likely to help you. You've probably learned the basics of good manners, but here's a quick recap:

- Say "please," "thank you," and "excuse me."
- Show concern for other people by asking how they are and what they are interested in, and listening to the answer.

- Never borrow things without asking first.
- Let people finish saying what they need to say without interruption.
- If you see somebody struggling, and it is safe to do so, ask if they need some help.

NATHAN SAYS...
I remember a time when I was struggling to make friends. At lunchtime I had no one to play with. I spent a lot of time playing on my own or sitting on the bench outside. I felt very miserable. After a while I spoke to my mom and the teachers. Once people knew how I felt and what was happening, they could help. My teachers began a buddy system, and my mom gave me some great advice: be true to myself and talk to people, showing an interest in what they are doing. I learned that usually people like to talk about themselves, so asking questions in an interested way and saying what you like about them can be a great icebreaker!

LISTENING

Listening does not mean hearing what somebody has said and then jumping in and talking about yourself. It means paying attention to what they are saying, listening to the words, and trying to understand the message they are trying to get across. Look at their face, nod your head, and respond to the person so they know they are being listened to.

BODY LANGUAGE

Good communication isn't just about what we say; it's also about how we say it. Our body language often makes more of an impact than the words we say. If you're speaking to somebody and they starting yawning and looking out of the window, it doesn't feel like they are listening, does it?

Your facial expressions, hand gestures, how fast or loud you talk, and the way you carry yourself send a message to the person you are communicating with. We need to get our body to match up with the words coming out of our mouth. It helps people to understand what we're trying to say and connect with us.

Pay attention to your body language when you're communicating with others. Here are some useful tips:

- Facial expressions—a smile is always nice, but it depends on the situation. If you hear some bad news then you wouldn't smile.

- A strong handshake when you meet somebody.

- Look people in the eye.

- Stand or sit up straight, with your shoulders back.

Taking the time to learn to listen properly with your eyes, ears, and body language will pay off in the long run-especially if you can repeat what you heard back and understand the other person's point of view.

SPEAKING

A great way to improve your communication skills is to learn how to speak to a group of people. You need to hold the audience's attention and put your points across in an interesting way so they understand what you're saying and remember it.

Imagine if two different people gave a talk. The first speaker asked you to stand up to practice your power poses, spoke loudly and confidently, and told you really interesting stories. The second person walked into the hall with their shoulders slumped, mumbled their message quietly, and didn't make eye contact or smile.

Which speaker would you listen to and remember? It'd be speaker number one, right? It's the person who related to you and gave an inspiring talk.

LEARNING PUBLIC SPEAKING

Some people can find public speaking really scary, but it's very useful to learn to improve your day-to-day communication skills and to add a skill to your toolkit. You may need to get out of your comfort zone, which is a good thing. You could ask your teacher or group leader if you could speak in front of the group.

DANIELLE SAYS...
I can clearly remember meeting Nathan for the first time because he made a fantastic impression. I was the guest speaker at an event and while I was setting up, he came over and introduced himself. He politely asked me how I was and then wanted to know whether I had written any books for children that could help him become the best he could be. When I said I hadn't, Nathan thought about it for a bit and then asked whether we could write one together. I was impressed with his confidence, clear communication, and ability to quickly think of solutions to a problem. Of course, I said yes—and I'm helping him with his public speaking too!

When you are speaking to a group:

Think about your message
Prepare the main points you want people to learn from your talk. Remember to keep them nice and simple.

Practice
Practice giving your talk in front of friends or family.

Deep breaths
Before you start speaking, think confidently and remember your positive affirmations—you're awesome and deserve to be treated with respect. Take a couple of deep breaths if you're feeling nervous.

Your voice
Speak clearly, loudly, and slowly so that everyone can hear you, and pause between sentences. Vary your voice to show different feelings, such as excitement, sadness, pride, and happiness.

Make it interesting
You could use photos or videos, tell stories or let the audience ask questions. You could have volunteers help you.

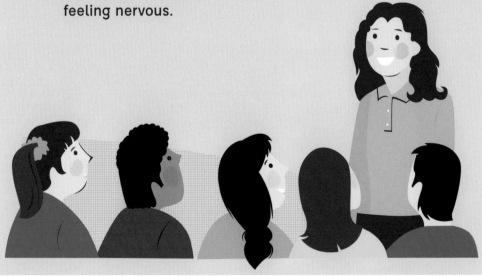

ROLE MODELS

You know what you want to achieve and it's time to put that plan into action. It will involve hard work, but you can get help from a role model. This is a person that inspires you and sets a good example.

We can learn a great deal from the people around us, following their lead, and copying their behavior. This is great if you have fantastic positive role models in your life, such as teachers, coaches, or community leaders. Bad role models exist too —people who make poor choices and behave badly. They may have achieved incredible things but without kindness or honesty.

By reading this book you have committed yourself to discovering the best version of yourself. If you look hard enough, you will find people who display the right sort of behavior and attitudes to make good role models. Role models can teach you how to achieve success and inspire you to keep going.

ROLE MODELS FOR SUCCESS

A good role model points you in the right direction and shows you the steps you need to take to achieve success. Instead of trying to figure out how to reach your goal all by yourself, do some research and find out who else has succeeded in the area you want to. You can learn what actions they took and the mistakes they made, which means that you are less likely to make the same ones.

DANIELLE SAYS... My parents told me that there was no such thing as "I can't" and whenever I found something difficult they would help me to keep going. This helped me later with some of the challenges I faced. Whenever I thought "this is too hard" or "I don't think I'm good enough to do this," I would remember what my parents taught me.

Be your best self

A RANGE OF ROLE MODELS

But, you might be thinking, what if what I want to achieve hasn't been done before?

Can a role model still help me? Yes! A role model doesn't give you a step-by-step guide to get from A to B. Successful people develop skills to help them reach their goals. Even if your goal has never been achieved before, you will need to master certain skills to reach it. There could be plenty of people out there who are excellent in those areas.

You can learn how to improve your skills from your role models. There probably won't be one person who is good at all the skills you want to gain, so learning from a few people who are fantastic at different skills helps you to become the best version of yourself. You might know somebody who is spectacularly confident. Another is very good at staying on track while a third person has excellent people skills.

If you know your role models, you can quiz them on the four questions in the box below, trying to find out as many details as possible. Be bold and ask them to help you draw up your road map or mentor you on your journey to success. Role models may be people you don't know. The Internet has turned the world into a small place, and you can learn about successful people if you do some research. If you can't find out the answers to your questions, try to reach out to them. They may not reply, but it's worth a try!

When you've found your role models, find out:

What did they do to achieve their success?
What important decisions did they make?
What skills and behaviors were important?
What mistakes did they make and how could they have been avoided?

INSPIRING YOU
TO KEEP GOING

Everybody has bad days and moments when they think they aren't good enough to achieve their goal. We all make mistakes and experience setbacks. When this happens, we may feel like giving up.

Even super-successful people make mistakes and experience ups and downs. You might think that they are perfect and that they achieved success because they are special. From the outside, it might look like their journey was easy. And sometimes, when you're at

the beginning of your own journey to success, it might feel as though the path in front of you is too hard and complicated.

We're going to let you in on a little secret now. Nobody on this planet is perfect, but every single human being is special and capable of achieving great things if they put their mind to it. Your role model most likely experienced setbacks and patches of bad luck. They probably hit times where it got really tough and they questioned whether they could carry on.

OVERCOMING SETBACKS

See if you can find somebody who has experienced major setbacks and learn what they did to get back on track. How do you think they felt when they faced this problem? And how did they manage to solve it? Can you imagine what they said to themselves in order to carry on? Sometimes hearing stories about others and how they overcame the struggles in their life can give us hope that the situation will improve. It can motivate us to keep going. If they found a way to do it, then you can too.

Remember, as much as good role models are important, nobody can be yourself better than you, so love and celebrate your true self. Shine, be happy, be confident–be the best you can be!

BUILDING YOUR SUPPORT TEAM

So far this book has been all about YOU. We've been looking at how you can become your best self—the most independent, resilient, and confident version of you. A big part of being brilliant is building a strong group of people around you who can help you succeed.

Your support team can help you through any challenges you might face, offering encouragement and advice. They guide you, build up your confidence and give you feedback to help you to improve. They motivate you when you are struggling to keep going and talk through any difficult decisions. Your support team can help you find opportunities to shine.

HOW TO BUILD A GREAT SUPPORT TEAM

Well, you've probably got some people in place already. You might get fantastic support from your family, friends, teachers, mentors, and advisors. Try to remember that while you are learning to be the best version of yourself, your supporters are learning how to be the best support

When you are trying to move mountains you want—and need—people on your side who want to move them with you.

JAMIE OLIVER

team they can be. Sometimes they get it wrong. So check if the people around you are giving you the right kind of support, and whether you need to expand your support team.

First, ask yourself: what do I want to achieve? This might be a HUGE goal or a rung on your stepladder to success (see page 18). Then ask: who can help me with this? For example, if you would like to learn to play a musical instrument, you need to find somebody with the right expertise who can teach you to play. Never be afraid to ask for help.

It is important to communicate well with your support team. They need to know how you like to receive feedback and what you really struggle to understand.

SAY YES TO OPPORTUNITIES

Opportunities are all around us. You might get the chance to learn a sport, a language, or to visit exciting places. Most of the time, saying "yes" to opportunities is a good idea. If you've never tried rock climbing before, you won't know if you like it until you give it a try.

Saying "yes" to an opportunity can be useful

- You never know what it will lead to—a small opportunity could turn into something bigger.
- It can help you develop skills.
- If it takes you out of your comfort zone, you will gain confidence.
- You'll meet new people and may make friends.

BAD OPPORTUNITIES

There is a big difference between saying "yes" to good opportunities and being pressured into doing something you don't want to do and won't benefit you. You'd be wise NOT to take up bad opportunities. They won't be of any benefit to you.

Here are some tips to help you decide if the opportunity is healthy:

Listen to your inner guiding voice. If something doesn't feel good, right, or safe to you, then it probably isn't. If you're unsure, ask a trusted adult for their advice.

Consider what this opportunity might mean for your goals and how you can take advantage of it. Does it relate to your short-term or long-term goals? When you're working toward a goal, sometimes an opportunity can help to make it happen.

Is it something you're interested in?

IDENTIFY OPPORTUNITIES

Opportunities aren't usually announced by flashing lights and sirens, or a knock on your door. Quite often, they come quietly, and in disguise, so it's good to always be ready. Flick the switch in your brain to "on" mode, and be on the lookout wherever you go for things that will help you achieve your goal. You can take many different routes to get where you want to go, so keep an open mind and explore all the options. Be curious and ask lots of questions. Then you'll be able to identify opportunities.

Opportunities don't always come along at the perfect moment—sometimes they happen when you least expect it! You might not feel ready to say "yes", but you never know when an opportunity like this will come along again. This is another great reason why it's important to keep your GOALS in mind—you never know when a lucky break might come your way.

Sometimes, rather than passively waiting for opportunities, you can be proactive and create opportunities for yourself.

All your dreams can come true if you have the courage to pursue them.
WALT DISNEY

Here are a few ideas for creating your own opportunities:

Take the time to try to find the right people who can help you.

If there is an event or exhibition that is relevant to your goal, try to go to it.

Develop your communication skills and talk about your goals to as many different people as possible. Make your voice heard and don't be afraid to ask questions.

Look at your goal-setting plan and write down the types of opportunities that will help you achieve it.

Be your best self

STAY MOTIVATED

When we decide we want to accomplish a goal, we need something to spur us on so we work hard and follow it through. This desire to keep going is our motivation. You need motivation to become good at all the skills we talk about in this book.

Some days this motivation comes easily—we feel excited and full of energy. On other days, we get distracted or the task in front of us looks too difficult and time-consuming. How can you keep your motivation levels high? If you're motivated by rewards, break a task down into small milestones and reward yourself when you reach each one, with a break to play or a snack. If competition excites you, try to beat your own scores or results.

> It always seems impossible until it is done.
>
> **NELSON MANDELA**

NATHAN SAYS...
I get a lot of motivation from my piano tutor, who tells me to keep focused, keep practicing, look at the notes, and not at my hands. Sometimes it's hard to stay motivated though. I remember when I had to learn a lot of difficult arpeggios, broken chords, and scales for Grade 3. It seemed boring practicing the same thing every day, and I couldn't stay motivated. This went on for over two weeks. Then I realized I had my exam soon and I risked failing! Now I had to practice more because I'd missed so much. I was inspired to work hard to pass the exam, and thankfully I did. It took some stress, effort, struggle, and serious motivation though!

What motivates you?
Think about what drives you, such as:

RESULTS
the feelings of satisfaction when you achieve a goal

RECOGNITION
being recognized by other people for your achievement

COMPETITION
competing against others or yourself

PERSONAL GROWTH
working hard so you are the best you can be

REWARDS
getting treats or awards for achieving something

PEOPLE
feeling a sense of belonging and being liked by others

FEAR
worrying about the consequences of failing

HELPING
making a difference to the world around you.

DANIELLE SAYS...
I am motivated by results. I like to set myself big, scary, and exciting goals that really push me. The thought of achieving gets me all fired up and I'm super motivated to put in all the work I need to get there. I've also been motivated by fear—I hate it when I fail at something so I work hard to reduce the risk of this happening. I love helping others so this is another important factor for me, and of course I like receiving awards! I'm motivated by competition, learning new skills, and being valued.

I make sure I do at least one thing every day to help me get closer to my goal. I use my motivations as fuel, so if I'm having a really bad day I can dig deep and find the strength and energy to keep going.

BOOST YOUR MOTIVATION
The ideas in this book can help to increase your drive.

For the difficult days

These ideas can help when you are lacking motivation:

Learning to be patient
It's important to stay on track and not give in to temptation.

How to keep going
A resilient mindset is important to help us through the tough times.

Learning how to fail well
Failure happens, but it's how you bounce back from it that counts.

Self-confidence
Trust your abilities. Know that you can deal with anything.

Role models
How do your role models deal with difficult days and stay motivated? Learning from our role models is a powerful tool.

Building your support team
They can help point you in the right direction and give you encouragement to keep going.

Self-worth
Remember you are loved and lovable and you are worth this!

Be your best self

EATING WELL

We all come in different shapes and sizes, but we all have the right to take care of ourselves in the best possible way. What you eat directly affects your health, confidence, intelligence, and mood. Good foods also help you sleep and make your immune system stronger. A healthy diet helps you to be the best you can be.

The healthiest foods are plants: fruits and vegetables in all of their colors, as well as seeds, nuts, beans, and lentils. It's best to eat them in as natural a state as possible. These nutritious foods make us feel alive and full of energy.

Why not turn healthy eating into a game? See how many fresh, natural foods in different colors you can eat in one day. The greater the variety, the better! Any vegetable or fruit is good—fresh, frozen, tinned, or dried.

Try to choose healthy snacks. Try fruit, nuts, vegetables and seeds, smoothies, or salads.

DANIELLE SAYS...
Eating the right food is an important part of an athlete's job. I used to have days when training had gone terribly and I wanted nothing more than to eat my favorite snacks. A little bit of what you crave now and then might not hurt. But making sure you don't do it too often is the key to good health. When I craved less healthy foods, I would think about my goals and ask myself, "Is this going to help me win gold?" The answer was NO of course, and this helped me stay motivated.

We should aim to eat *at least* ten portions of fruit and vegetables a day. There are tremendous health benefits to this diet:

It prevents serious diseases like heart disease, strokes, and cancer.

You are far less likely to carry extra weight on your body.

It gives you much more energy.

You will feel happier and healthier.

It will help with conditions like eczema or pimples and improve your skin.

Fruit and vegetables are good for your digestive system.

You are likely to live longer.

Be your best self

FAT IN FOOD

People often think that fat in our diet is bad. You've probably seen food packets that say "fat free" or "low in fat." But low-fat foods are often high in sugar. And guess what your body turns sugar into? Fat! "Low fat" usually means "more processed," and processed foods often contain salt and other unhealthy ingredients.

Now here's the scientific part: your brain needs fat to function. Some fats are bad for you, while others are good. Helpful fats are in nuts, seeds, avocado, egg, extra virgin olive oil, coconut oil, fish, and dark chocolate. Bad fats are found in cakes, chocolate, processed foods, chips, and margarine.

GOOD FATS

BAD FATS

NATHAN SAYS...

When I was a baby I had pretty bad eczema. Doctors gave me creams, ointments, and medicines. I sometimes even had to sleep wrapped in plastic wrap, but nothing really helped. This is when my mom took a real interest in nutrition. What she found out changed my life. We stopped all white bread, pasta and rice, dairy products, and processed foods. We began to eat LOTS of fruit and vegetables in every meal.

As well as treating my body well from the inside, we switched to organic oils and kinder bath products for the outside. After ten weeks of a healthy diet, my eczema almost disappeared. Now, several years later, I LOVE healthy nutrition—it's definitely part of me being the best I can be. I'd choose a ripe and juicy passion fruit over fast-food fries any day.

Instead of feeling unlucky for getting eczema if I eat junk food, I feel happy that my body gives me instant signs to stop if I have it. It's like I have super powers—a built-in Junk-o-meter! If I consume anything that's not good for me, my skin tells me so that I can learn from it. Most people aren't lucky enough to get that warning, so I feel grateful that I do. I always check in and listen to my body.

SLEEP AND SUCCESS

If you want to be the very best you can be, it's vital to get a good night's sleep. Sleeping lets us recharge our batteries so we have plenty of energy, we can concentrate and our memory works well.

Don't worry if you're not a great sleeper. First, take a look at your sleep routine. Do you get up and go to bed at the same time every day? Sticking to a routine improves the quality of your sleep, so you wake up feeling nice and refreshed. You might want to stay up a bit later or sleep in a little longer on the weekends or during school breaks, but try to keep to this routine whenever you can.

PREPARE FOR BED

Before you go to bed, you can prepare yourself for sleep. Turn off the TV, computer, tablet, or phone AT LEAST an hour before bedtime. The light in a screen keeps your brain awake, which makes getting to sleep much more difficult. It also stops the brain from producing melatonin, the chemical that it needs to fall asleep. A dark room is the best place to fall asleep, so turn off all the lights.

In that hour before you go to sleep, there are plenty of things you can do to help you relax:

Enjoy a warm bath

Have a warm drink (without caffeine)

Read a book

Listen to an audio book

Draw or do some artwork

Listen to relaxing music

Do some gentle exercises.

Be your best self

Having a sleep routine sets your body clock.
Your body will start to get sleepy at the same
time each evening and become more alert
at the same time in the morning.

THE NIGHT BEFORE A BIG DAY

Sometimes if we feel a bit anxious or excited about a big day ahead, it can be difficult to fall asleep. Our mind stays active and we feel wide awake. Has this ever happened to you?

Try to figure out what is keeping you from sleeping. Are you feeling a bit worried? If so, talking about the problem with a parent or friend is a good idea. They might be able to reassure you or offer support and advice. Some people find it helps to write down what's on their mind.

Even if you don't feel sleepy, it's important to stick to your bedtime routine. Before you go to bed, make sure you have everything ready for the next day. It will give you some peace of mind and mean that you're not rushing around like a tornado in the morning.

RELAXATION

Now it's time to get your body to relax. Telling yourself to relax doesn't usually work, but there is a quick and easy way to relax your body. It's called Progressive Muscle Relaxation, or PMR for short.

Start at the bottom of your body and clench your toes as tightly as you can for five seconds.

Relax your toes and breathe out at the same time. You will breathe out all the tension that was in your toes. Work your way up through your body. Tense up your legs, stomach, back, arms, neck, and jaw, and then let go.

Once you've finished, your whole body should feel much more relaxed. You might have to repeat PMR a few times before your body is ready for sleep.

DANIELLE SAYS... I always wanted to perform at my very best in competitions and this meant that I got both nervous and excited the night before. As soon as I climbed into bed, I would imagine the competition and how I was going to do, my heart thumping loudly in my chest. It was really difficult to get these images out of my mind and I struggled to get to sleep, which made me even more frustrated! I knew how important sleep was—if I was tired I wasn't going to be at my very best. After learning how to relax better and calm my thoughts, I found it much easier to get to sleep the night before an important match. This meant that I was full of energy the next day and ready to give it my all.

BEING ACTIVE

You might be wondering what exercise has to do with helping you to be your best self. Being the best you can be is not just about practicing the skills that train your brain, like confidence or communication. Your brain lives in your body, so you need to make sure it works as well as possible.

Research shows that when children exercise regularly, their well-being and even their IQ can increase, too.

Why is exercise so important?

It helps you focus better

Improves your memory

Increases the size of your brain

Gives you more energy

Puts you in a better mood

Helps prevent illness

Is an excellent way to make new friends.

The best part is that sports can be fun. Some of you will be nodding your heads, because you already take part in regular exercise and really enjoy it. Keep up the awesome work! But some of you will have a horrible sinking feeling in your stomach. You might be thinking, "Well, that counts me out. I'm terrible at sports and I hate them!"

This doesn't have to mean that you can't enjoy sports or be good at them. There is a type of exercise out there for everybody. You might not have found the right one for you yet.

Some people worry that spending time exercising will be bad for their studies. In fact, it will help you learn better. It's good to give your brain a break. When you come in, you will feel fresh and ready to study again.

DANIELLE SAYS...

My disability means that my feet hurt all the time. For me, running is impossible and walking is difficult so I can't take part in many sports. I looked around for a sport that didn't involve lots of running around and walking, and archery sounded fun. I joined an archery club on my 15th birthday and I was absolutely terrible at first. This didn't matter. I enjoyed myself so much that I kept pestering my mom and dad to take me to training. The more I practiced, the better I got; the better I got, the more I enjoyed

 it; and the more I enjoyed it, the more I wanted to practice. I never thought in a million years that I'd become an athlete and represent my country, but I just happened to find the right sport for me!

Be your best self

FINDING OUT WHAT YOU ENJOY

How do you find the right sport? First, look at the reasons why you don't enjoy it. Do any of these reasons apply to you? "I'm bad at it, I don't feel confident, I had a bad experience and it put me off."

Now you can start doing something about it. Remember that growth mindset—we can learn any skill when we put our mind to it. It takes some people longer to master things than others. Don't compare yourself to others—monitor your own progress and see whether you are improving.

Confidence is one of our key skills—see page 50 for tips to help you build it up. Remember that going outside your comfort zone is a big part of becoming more confident. It's horrible to have a bad experience, but don't let it turn you off sports completely. Not all sports are the same, and the next sport you try might be great fun. Now think about the sports that you: absolutely hate, find OK, enjoy a little, and enjoy a lot.

What was it about these sports that you didn't enjoy? What made some sports OK? And what would have made you enjoy a sport even more? Now compare lots of sports to see if you can find one that might suit you.

Getting out there

Some people enjoy sports but are not motivated to practice. They would rather play video games or watch TV. If this sounds like you, here are a few suggestions for getting a healthy dose of exercise.

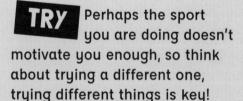 **TRY** Perhaps the sport you are doing doesn't motivate you enough, so think about trying a different one, trying different things is key!

TRY Invite your friends to do sports with you, or join them in their activities. Going to sports classes and playing team sports are great opportunities to make new friends too.

TRY Build exercise into your daily routine—maybe you could walk or bike to school or other places.

Taking part in sports will help you practice all of the skills in this book and help you become the best you can be.

PRACTICE YOUR SUCCESS SKILLS

This book is packed full of strategies to help you become the best version of yourself. You've been given exercises and suggestions for each one. With practice, they will help you become the best version of yourself and take you one step closer to achieving your dreams. There is another way to practice these success skills—by playing sports.

Sports teach you about drive, hard work, and sticking to your goals. They teach you how to be a member of a team and to communicate well with others. Sports develop your thinking and leadership skills. You learn about taking responsibility, competition, fair play, and respect. You practice setting goals and working on the tasks that will help you reach them. It's also a fantastic way to build confidence—to stretch your comfort zone, learn new skills, and take pride in your achievements.

LEARNING FROM FAILURE

And you learn a lot about failure. It happens a lot in sport—sometimes you are unlucky, make mistakes, or don't play to the best of your ability, or you're outmatched by a better team. Each failure is an opportunity to learn, helping you develop resilience and a positive attitude. It teaches you to dig a little deeper and push a little further, and learn that there is always a path to success, no matter how hard it is to find.

With all these benefits, it's an instant win. So call your friends, go outside and play some sports. And remember, sports should be fun, so make sure you're doing something you enjoy.

Failing is a crucial part of success. Every time you fail and get back up, you practice perseverance, which is the key to life. Your strength comes in your ability to recover.
MICHELLE OBAMA

OVER TO YOU

Life is a journey, full of twists and turns. There are many ups and downs, excitements, challenges, boring parts, and failures. Life can sometimes seem tough, while at other times we are given extraordinary opportunities.

Whenever you set out on a journey it's important to be prepared. That's exactly what this book is for. Each chapter has covered important skills that you can take on your journey to success. They help you to navigate tricky ground, make the most of your strengths, and grow through your weaknesses.

You see, even small steps take us somewhere. By doing one thing each day, whether it's practicing visualization, getting organized, or saying kind words to yourself, you are building useful habits. Over time, you won't have to think about it anymore. You will stop trying and start BEING your best self.

And remember, success isn't handed to us on a plate. Life doesn't give us quick wins and easy solutions. Sometimes, it might feel like you're working harder than everybody else or not improving as quickly, but that's OK. We all work at our own pace. We're all great at many things but we all need help with others.

Now it's over to you. You've learned the ideas behind success and being your best self so now it's time to put them into practice. Remember, success happens one step at a time... One mindful action, one choice at a time. So, work at these strategies and try one thing each day that will help you become the best you can be.

Just one thing! That's it!

You deserve success

Keep on working on yourself, keep aiming for success—whatever success means to you—and learn to love and appreciate yourself for the wonderful person you are. That's right, you are. Say it. Say it again. You deserve this. You are unique and special, and you have the ability to deal with anything that comes your way. Everything you want to be you already are. You just need to practice.

You have come to the end of this book, but you are at the start of your journey and we wish you lots of happiness and success. Dream big, work hard, and never give up. You are worth it!

ABOUT THE AUTHORS

Nathan Kai pioneered then jointly wrote this book when he was only seven years old. Why? Because this AMAZING book should have been on the shelves, and he desperately wanted to have it for Christmas, but it didn't exist (then...). He's a member of MENSA, is the world's youngest published self-development author, a public motivational speaker, and an elite athlete (a multi-National and European Champion medalist in jiu-jitsu). He's also a talented pianist, child model, linguist, and a thoroughly awesome person. He's delighted that the book is out for you to learn these tips for success and happiness and to Go On and BE YOUR BEST SELF!

Danielle Brown MBE Danielle Brown MBE is a double Paralympic gold medalist and five-time World Champion in archery. She was World Number One for her entire career and made history when she became the first disabled athlete to represent England in an able-bodied discipline at the Commonwealth Games. Danielle now works as a keynote speaker and specializes in self-development, success skills, and breaking through barriers. She does a lot of work with young people to help them improve their academic performance and mental well-being. www.daniellebrown.co.uk

Authors' acknowledgements

In this book we talk about the importance of having a good support team, and we are no different. We have built an amazing support team around us in order to write this book and ensure it is the very best it can be. One person deserves an extra special mention: Anna Kai, Nathan's mom, is a psychotherapist and nutritionist and has been instrumental in the development of *Be Your Best Self.* Her knowledge and experience in child development and psychology has proved invaluable, not to mention her love, devotion, and encouragement for her amazing children and the people around her.

In memory of beautiful Louisa "Nana" Bleasdale Bonney. You meant more than words can say: a compass and oar through rocky waters. A haven. A source of unconditional love, and you will be remembered ad infinitum. You were right.

We take our time to love, remember, and pay respects to our ancestors who we have loved and lost. We also want to thank our amazing families and friends who have stuck with us, empowered us, and encouraged us to turn our visions into realities. Without your loyalty and support, we would not be where we are now. With immense thanks, and love.

Martin and Liz Power, devoted piano teachers and tutors. They have been a rock to Nathan and to them we are immensely grateful. All of Nathan's professors, coaches, and supporters in jiu-jitsu—OSSS! Thank you to you all. You know who you are. We love you.

We hope you can see and enjoy these beautiful words come to fruition and help others. Thank you. Just thank you! We love you.

Picture credits

All illustrations by Joanna Kerr except pages 1, 2, 3, 4, 5, 7, 12, 14, 16, 24, 25, 26, 28, 29, 38, 41, 46, 47, 49, 58, 62, 63, 64, 66, 67 (bottom), 71, 72, 81, 84, 90, 91, 94, 105, 106, 114, 119, and 120 from Shutterstock.com

Be your best self

INDEX

First published 2020 by
Guild of Master Craftsman Publications Ltd
Castle Place, 166 High Street, Lewes,
East Sussex BN7 1XU

Text © Danielle Brown and Nathan Kai, 2020
Copyright in the Work © GMC Publications Ltd,
2020

ISBN 978 1 78708 039 3

Publisher Jonathan Bailey
Production Jim Bulley, Jo Pallett
Editor Cath Senker
Managing Art Editor Gilda Pacitti
Art Editor Cathy Challinor
Illustrator Joanna Kerr

Color origination by GMC Reprographics
Printed and bound in China

For more on Button Books, contact:
GMC Publications Ltd, Castle Place,
166 High Street, Lewes, East Sussex,
BN7 1XU, United Kingdom
Tel: +44 (0)1273 488005
www.buttonbooks.co.uk